Flowerscape

IN PARADISE

A TROPICAL COLORING BOOK

BY MAGGIF ENTERRIOS

PAGE STREET
PUBLISHING CO.

PAGE STREET
PUBLISHING CO.

First published in 2023 by
Page Street Publishing Co.
27 Congress Street, Suite 1511
Salem, MA 01970
www.pagestreetpublishing.com

Distributed by Macmillan, sales in Canada by The Canadian Manda Group.

27   26   25   24   23   2   3   4   5

ISBN-13: 978-1-62414-912-2
ISBN-10: 1-62414-912-X

Illustrations and cover design by Maggie Enterrios
Cover lettering by Adé Hogue

Printed and bound in China

THIS BOOK BELONGS TO

FLOWERSCAPE IN PARADISE

INTRODUCTION

Embrace your wanderlust. *Flowerscape in Paradise* is an adventure for your creativity: a celebration of the beautiful botanical and animal life that we dream of exploring. Perfumed flowers dance across the page, awaiting your hand to bring them to life in new and unique ways. Bold patterns and geometric elements echo the tapestries, weavings and tilework that you may envision as you wander through jungles, beaches and tropical destinations around the world.

As I illustrated this book, I fondly remembered all of the places I've been fortunate enough to visit, and imagined all of the places I hope to someday see. Much like travel, creativity is a tool that allows you to broaden your horizons, unwind and explore new ideas.

There is nothing quite so magical as being whisked away, whether that's in person or simply through the act of creating art. No matter where you are, let *Flowerscape in Paradise* take you on a vacation.

Share your art online by following @colorflowerscape and tagging #flowerscapeinparadise!

FLOWER IDENTIFICATION

There are no rules when it comes to coloring this book. Neon orchids?
Go for it! Rainbow dahlias? Give it a try! Let your imagination run wild.

For those of you who prefer some color palette recommendations,
Flowerscape in Paradise has a treasure trove of resources available.
On the left-hand side of each spread, you'll find sample illustrations of
the main botanicals used in each composition. Simply open your cam-
era app on your smartphone, and hover it over the QR code on any
flower identification page in this book. Center the QR code within the
screen, and you'll be automatically linked to the corresponding color
key for each design. You'll get a quick and easy reference so you can
jump right back into coloring . . . without the guesswork.

Alternatively, you can access all of the book's color keys, as well as
free printable coloring pages and an inspiration gallery, by visiting
colorflowerscape.com/paradise or by scanning the QR code below.

clivia

torch ginger

kiwi blossom

porcelain flower

anthurium

blue star fern

protea

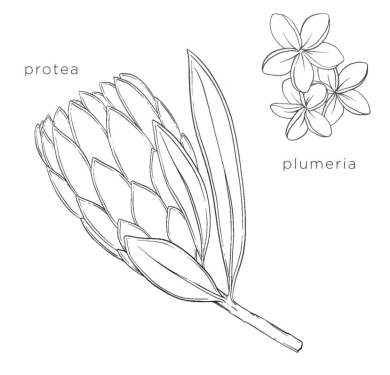

plumeria

kaleidoscope
orchid

pentas

waxflower

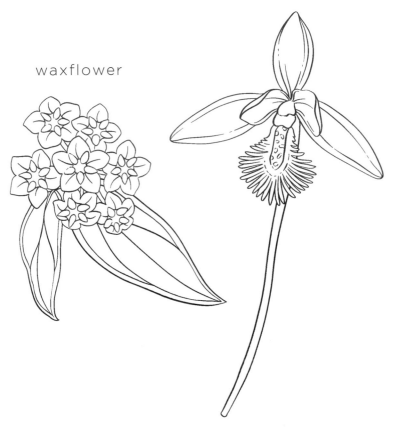

rose pogonia

passionflower

bleeding heart vine

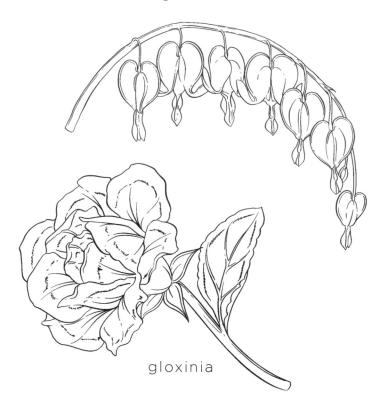

gloxinia

sasanqua

wattle

blue plumbago

camellia

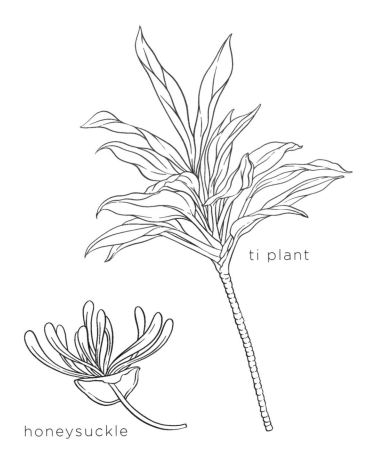

ti plant

honeysuckle

scan here for
color reference

lobster claws

queen's wreath

scarlet star

rocktrumpet

giant waxflower

african iris

spotted begonia

begonia blossom

flannel flower

waratah

scan here for
color reference

rosy periwinkle

laelia orchid

aerangis orchid

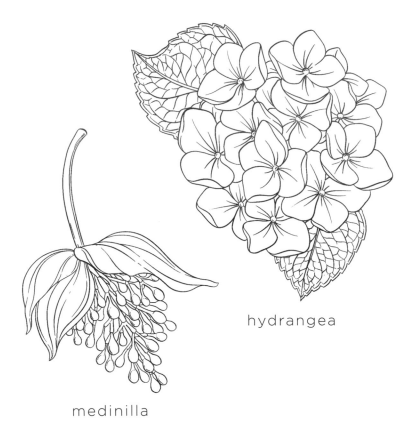

hydrangea

medinilla

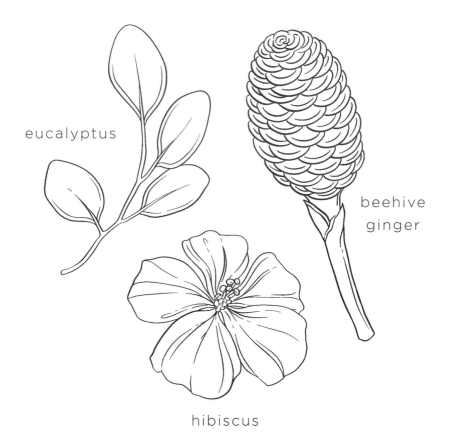

eucalyptus

beehive
ginger

hibiscus

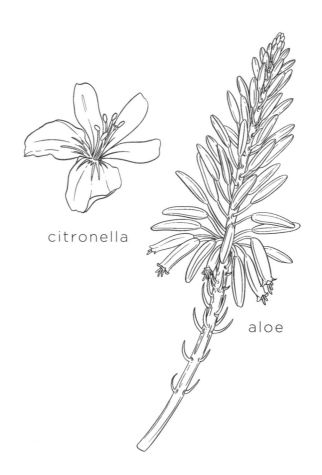

citronella

aloe

sandpaper vine

mile-a-minute flower

bird of paradise

scan here for
color reference

moth orchid

blue lily

pinwheel plumeria

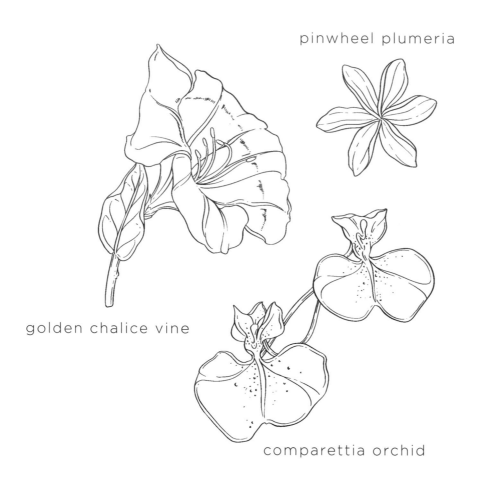

golden chalice vine

comparettia orchid

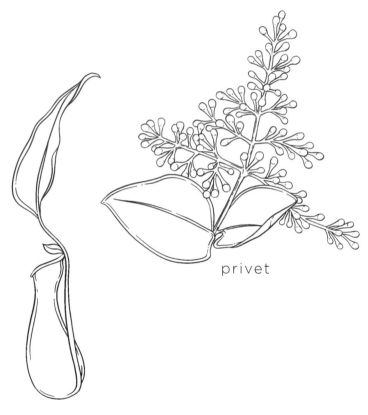

privet

pitcher plant

scan here for
color reference

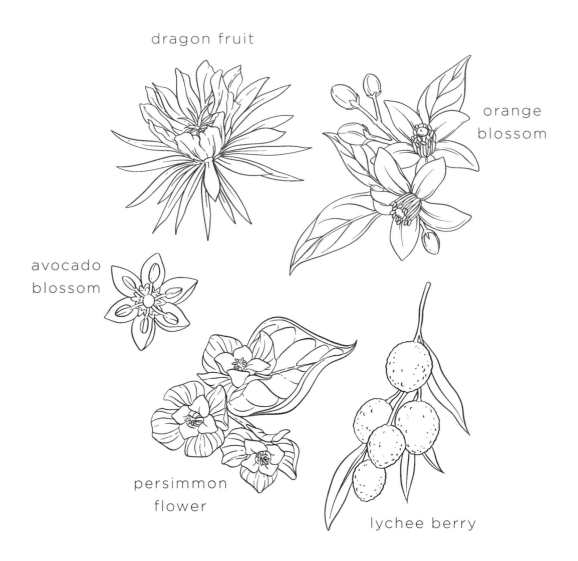

dragon fruit

orange
blossom

avocado
blossom

persimmon
flower

lychee berry

aeonium

coral bells
succulent

scan here for
color reference

crimson cattleya

canna lily

begonia flower

blue tango

pomegranate blossom

scan here for
color reference

hibiscus

kaneohe sunburst

scan here for
color reference

lime blossom

angel's trumpet

boat orchid

impala lily

scan here for
color reference

heliconia

bower vine

rocktrumpet

plumeria

begonia leaf

water lily

dwarf lotus

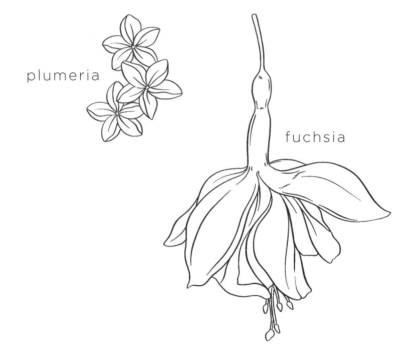

plumeria

fuchsia

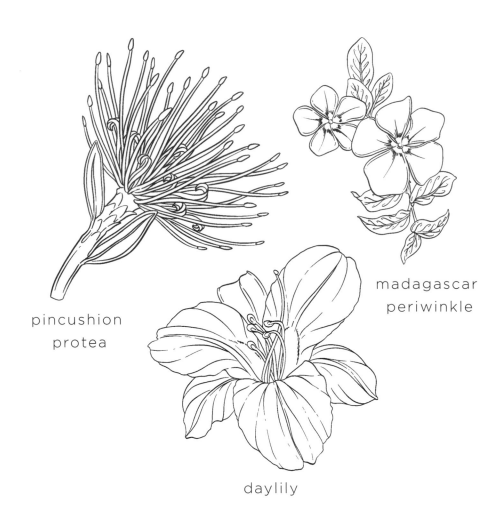

pincushion
protea

madagascar
periwinkle

daylily

jasmine

red ginger

dahlia

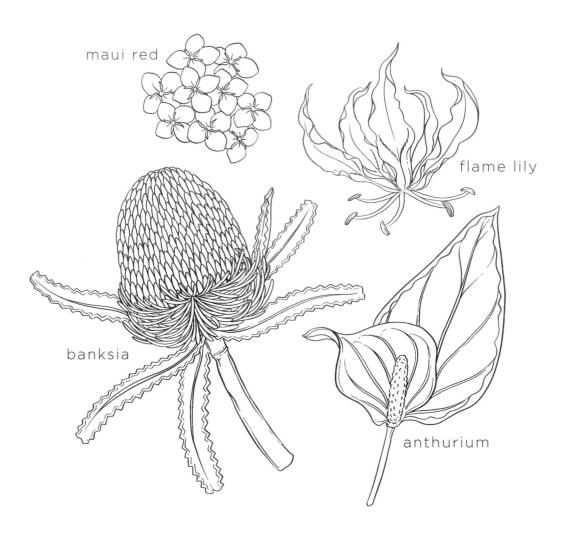

maui red

flame lily

banksia

anthurium

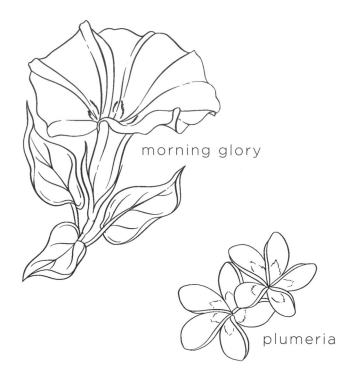

morning glory

plumeria

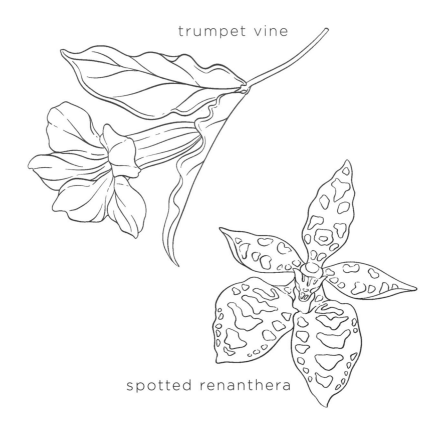

trumpet vine

spotted renanthera

oleander

flowering maple

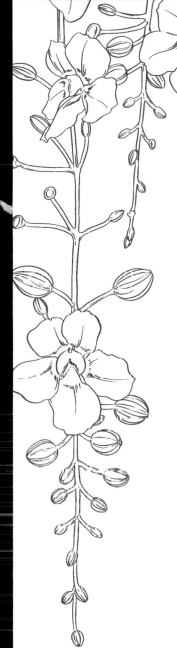

ABOUT THE ARTIST

Maggie Enterrios is a commercial illustrator most known for her intricate botanical drawings, packaging designs, fabrics and editorial artwork. *Flowerscape in Paradise* is Maggie's second coloring book, following on the heels of her debut book, *Flowerscape* (2021). She is humbled by the warm welcome that the coloring community has shown her, and hopes that this book serves as a token of her deep appreciation.

Many of the plants featured in this book are inspired by Maggie's travels, especially through Hawaii, where her family has deep roots, and Australia. During her travels, she enjoys walking in nature, visiting botanical gardens and sketching plants. More of her artwork can be found at www.littlepatterns.com and across social media @littlepatterns.

When she is not creating art, Maggie spends her time outside, but is more inclined to lounging than adventuring. She enjoys taking naps, preferably in a hammock or while floating in an inner tube on a lake. She adores her dog, Willie, and spends a fair amount of time teaching him new tricks.

SPECIAL THANKS

Maggie would like to extend an overarching thank you to all of the friends who have ever taken a walk with her, and apologizes for the frequent and abrupt stops they've been forced to make in order for her to photograph flowers. To her mom, Lucile, for teaching her to love doodling. To Angelika Piwowarczyk, for researching and coloring every single flower identification page. To her husband, Adam, whose unwavering support has single-handedly made all of this (and everything in their lives) possible. And to her friend, Adé Hogue, who designed the *Flowerscape* cover lettering. She misses him dearly, and every rose that she draws is for him.

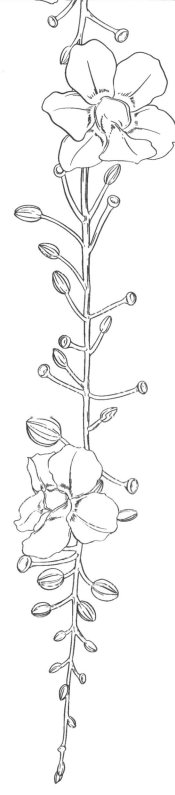